W9-BFT-936

# WORLD WAR I CAUSES

ESSENTIAL LIBRARY OF
# WORLD WAR I

Essential Library

An Imprint of Abdo Publishing
abdopublishing.com

## BY NATHAN SACKS

### CONTENT CONSULTANT

STEVE SABOL
ASSOCIATE PROFESSOR OF HISTORY
UNIVERSITY OF NORTH CAROLINA AT CHARLOTTE

abdopublishing.com

Published by Abdo Publishing, a division of ABDO, PO Box 398166, Minneapolis, Minnesota 55439. Copyright © 2016 by Abdo Consulting Group, Inc. International copyrights reserved in all countries. No part of this book may be reproduced in any form without written permission from the publisher. Essential Library™ is a trademark and logo of Abdo Publishing.

Printed in the United States of America, North Mankato, Minnesota

102015
012016

Cover Photo: The Art Archive/SuperStock
Interior Photos: The Art Archive/SuperStock, 1; Bettmann/Corbis, 4, 64; Picture-Alliance/DPA/AP Images, 7; H.-D. Falkenstein/ImageBROKER RM/Glow Images, 9, 29, 99 (top); Red Line Editorial, 10, 11; iStockphoto, 12; SuperStock/Glow Images, 16, 42, 98 (top), 98 (bottom); akg-images/Newscom, 21, 24, 39, 40, 46, 52, 57, 60, 72, 83, 86; The Print Collector/Heritage Images/Glow Images, 23; Deposit Photos/Glow Images, 27, 33, 45; adoc-photos/Corbis, 34; Mondadori/Newscom, 51; Everett Collection/Newscom, 54; Leemage/UIG/Getty Images, 62; Europics/Newscom, 69; Wikimedia Commons, 71; AP Images, 75, 99 (bottom); Ann Ronan Pictures/Heritage Images/Glow Images, 78; DPA/Picture-Alliance/DPA/AP Images, 80; Mirrorpix/Newscom, 89, 90; Elzbieta Sekowska/Shutterstock Images, 93; Shutterstock Images, 97

Editor: Nick Rebman
Series Designers: Kelsey Oseid and Maggie Villaume

Library of Congress Control Number: 2015945649

Cataloging-in-Publication Data

Sacks, Nathan.
 World War I causes / Nathan Sacks.
  p. cm. -- (Essential library of World War I)
 ISBN 978-1-62403-928-7 (lib. bdg.)
 Includes bibliographical references and index.
 1. World War, 1914-1918--Causes--Juvenile literature.  2. Arms race--Europe--History--20th century--Juvenile literature.   I. Title.
940.3/11--dc23

                                             2015945649

# CONTENTS

Franz Ferdinand and his wife, Sophie, were in Bosnia to observe military maneuvers of the Austro-Hungarian army.

# THE POWDER KEG

Surrounded by the citizens of Sarajevo, Bosnia, a young man named Gavrilo Princip stood along a road waiting for a motorcade to pass by. It was June 28, 1914, and the crowd had gathered to see Archduke Franz Ferdinand, heir to the throne of the Austro-Hungarian Empire. Unlike most of the other people in the crowd, Princip was not there to cheer the leader. He had a different purpose—and he had a pistol in his pocket.

In addition to Princip, five other young assassins stood along the vehicle's path, each armed with a gun, a grenade, or both. These men, along with a few other conspirators, had spent months planning for this day. Franz Ferdinand was everything these young radicals hated. He was a royalist and an elitist. Furthermore, he represented the interests of Austria-Hungary. To the frustration

## THE BALKANS

The Balkan Peninsula is a region in southeastern Europe bordered by the Adriatic Sea to the west, the Aegean Sea to the south, and the Black Sea to the east. The region is commonly known as the Balkans. Today, it includes the nations of Bosnia and Herzegovina, Montenegro, and Serbia. But for the decades leading up to World War I, these areas were controlled by various imperial powers, including Austria-Hungary and the Ottoman Empire.

of Bosnian Serbs such as Princip and the other assassins, Austria-Hungary had annexed the province of Bosnia from the Ottoman Empire in 1908.

Though the archduke's path through Sarajevo had been published in newspapers months ago, Princip did not know whether he would have a shot at Franz Ferdinand that day. There had already been one unsuccessful attempt on the archduke's life earlier that morning. But the other assassins had missed their chances; one managed to throw a bomb, but it damaged a car behind the archduke, causing no casualties. After that, local security forces quickly whisked the statesman inside the town hall and planned an escape route.

Franz Ferdinand's security team changed the archduke's route out of the city. At first, they drove out of town quickly, making it difficult for any would-be gunmen to take aim. But one of the drivers did not know about the alternate route. After crossing a bridge, the confused driver came to a stop right in front of Gavrilo Princip, who found himself within a few feet of the man he had come to kill.

Princip raised his pistol. The archduke's driver saw the gun and tried to back up the car. The engine stalled, and the car did not move. A man tried to shield the archduke and his wife, but he was on the other side of the car. Princip had a clear line of sight, and he fired twice. The first bullet hit Franz Ferdinand in the neck. The second shot hit the archduke's wife, Sophie, in the abdomen. Both died.

## DIPLOMATIC MISSTEPS LEAD TO CONFLICT

The assassination of Archduke Franz Ferdinand set in motion a flurry of diplomatic actions across Europe. Believing Serbia was responsible for

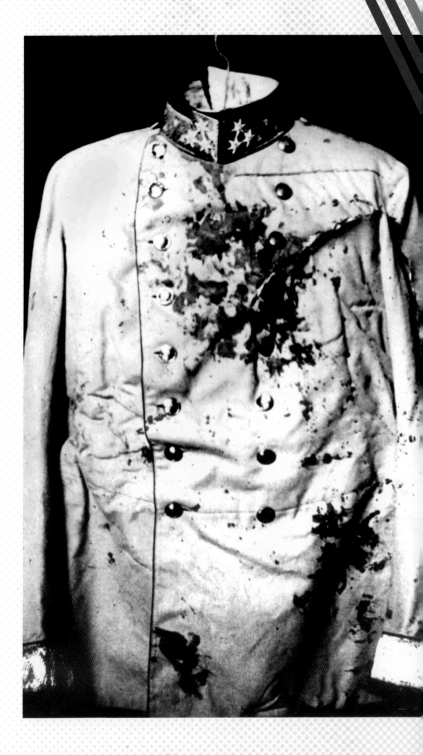

Franz Ferdinand's uniform was covered in blood after the assassination.

the assassination, Austria-Hungary reached out to Germany for advice on how to respond. Germany's leader, Kaiser Wilhelm II, encouraged Austria-Hungary to deal harshly with Serbia in retaliation for the assassination. But Wilhelm II believed a solution could be reached without bloodshed. In reality, however, Austria-Hungary planned to go to war with Serbia. Wilhelm II pledged Germany's support to Austria-Hungary, but he did not realize doing so would lead his country into war as well.

Serbia, fearing an attack from Austria-Hungary, immediately sought the help of its ally Russia. Russian leader Czar Nicholas II advised Serbia to mobilize its military. On July 28, Austria-Hungary declared war on Serbia. In support of Serbia, Russia prepared to mobilize its own military.

In the days that followed, Germany's leaders debated how to respond to Russia's mobilization. This situation posed a double threat to Germany. Germany's alliance with Austria-Hungary meant Germany would come to the aid of Austria-Hungary if Russia declared war. But Russia was also an ally of France, which bordered Germany in the west. Therefore, German

## WILLY-NICKY TELEGRAMS

Wilhelm II, the leader of Germany, and Nicholas II, the leader of Russia, were third cousins. The two leaders maintained friendly communication during the diplomatic crisis in 1914 that eventually led to war. They signed telegrams as "Willy" and "Nicky" while their countries prepared for conflict.[1] When war seemed imminent, Wilhelm II sent his cousin a telegram pleading with him to stop the full mobilization of Russian troops. The note worked, but only for a day.

leaders worried war with Russia would also bring war with France.

Russia refused to stop the mobilization of its troops. So, on August 1, Germany declared war on Russia. Two days later, Germany declared war on Russia's ally France. Only a week later, Belgium and the United Kingdom had also joined the war, siding with Russia and France. World War I had begun.

Wilhelm II ruled Germany from 1888 to 1918.

# EUROPEAN BORDERS
## BEFORE AND AFTER WORLD WAR I

**ALLIES**
**CENTRAL POWERS**
**NEUTRAL**

NORWAY
SWEDEN
DENMARK
NETHERLANDS
GERMANY
RUSSIA
UNITED KINGDOM
BELGIUM
LUXEMBOURG
AUSTRIA-HUNGARY
FRANCE
SWITZERLAND
ROMANIA
ITALY
SERBIA
MONTENEGRO
BULGARIA
ALBANIA
SPAIN
GREECE
PORTUGAL
OTTOMAN EMPIRE
ALGERIA
TUNISIA
MOROCCO
LIBYA
EGYPT

1914

# 1921

After World War I ended in 1918, smaller wars continued in eastern Europe. By 1921, European borders were relatively stable and remained in place until World War II began in the late 1930s.

During the Industrial Revolution, steam-powered machines enabled workers to manufacture goods more efficiently.

# THE PEOPLE RISE, MONARCHIES DECLINE

Throughout the 1800s, the nations of Europe enjoyed a rapid increase in technological developments. Today, this period is known as the Industrial Revolution. Between the mid-1700s and the mid-1800s, the invention of power-driven machines, the steam engine, and industrialized factories changed the fabric of society. The standard of living rose for many workers who used their newfound freedom to argue for better wages and more rights.

With these economic improvements came the desire to change how countries were governed. When World War I began in 1914, France was the only completely democratic republic in Europe. All other major powers were ruled by monarchies. Some monarchs,

## THE INDUSTRIAL REVOLUTION

The Industrial Revolution began in approximately 1760 in the United Kingdom. By the 1800s, it was spreading through the rest of Europe. In the span of only a few decades, new technologies had transformed agriculture, energy production, transportation, and communication. The invention of iron and steel made heavy equipment—such as locomotives, power looms, and the internal combustion engine—possible and popular. With the rapid growth in technology came equally dramatic social changes. Workers began leaving farms and moving to cities for jobs, manufacturing, and trade. And once workers began making more money, many desired more say in local and national politics.

such as Czar Nicholas II of Russia, wielded nearly total control over their countries in foreign, domestic, and military matters. Others, such as King George V of the United Kingdom, shared power with an elected parliament.

As the 1800s progressed, the average income and standard of living increased for workers throughout the world, creating a new middle class. With newfound economic power, the middle class began demanding more political power, which previously had been reserved for nobility and royalty. In 1848, revolutions broke out across Europe, as did waves of patriotism and the wish for self-rule. Monarchs gradually conceded more power to the people, creating tension within countries that were also trying to maintain their status as players on the world stage. The waves of nationalism rippling across the continent, combined with the changing balance of power within nations, created a situation ripe for international conflict.

## THE DUAL MONARCHY

Franz Ferdinand was one of the last members of a prestigious royal family. The Hapsburg family's roots were so deep in history they stretched back almost 1,000 years. Despite its centuries-long history of incredible power, the Hapsburg family would find its influence extinguished after World War I.

Between 1452 and 1806, the Hapsburgs dominated through military conquest and careful marriages calculated for maximum political gain. Soon, they had kingdoms throughout Europe and beyond. By the mid-1800s, however, the Hapsburgs had lost control over much of their territory, only maintaining power over the states of Austria and Hungary. In 1867, Austrian emperor Franz Joseph became emperor of both Austria and Hungary. These two Hapsburg-controlled territories would be ruled as one great country, a dual monarchy called the Austro-Hungarian Empire. Combining the two countries

### ENLIGHTENMENT THINKERS

In the 1700s, thinkers such as Jean-Jacques Rousseau, Voltaire, and Thomas Jefferson wrote about the inherent individual dignity and rights of humans. Generally, Enlightenment thinkers believed humans could use reason to improve their lives and their societies, and that obtaining knowledge, happiness, and freedom should be major goals of people and civilizations. Greater literacy and lower printing costs in the 1800s made the ideas of Enlightenment thinkers widely available. Mass production of books, pamphlets, and newspapers put these ideas in the hands of the poor, the working class, and the middle class. These groups soon began demanding more influence in how their governments operated.

would help the new empire maintain its status as an imperial power.

Though this arrangement helped Austria-Hungary remain a player on the world stage, the rulers' power at home was beginning to wane. During the Industrial Revolution, the Hapsburg dynasty became a victim of shifting divisions in society. Students demonstrated in the streets of Vienna, Austria, on March 13, 1848, to demand basic freedoms for the people of Austria and changes to the system of government. The unrest lasted until October 31, when the Austrian army took control of the city by force, executing some of the leaders of the revolution.

Franz Joseph was the longest-reigning emperor of Austria. He ruled from 1848 to 1916.

Though the monarchy maintained control of the empire, the events of 1848 sparked feelings of nationalism in the various groups within Austria-Hungary. These groups included Austrians, Hungarians, Serbians, Croatians, Slovaks, and Romanians. Nationalistic feelings continued after the creation of Austria-Hungary in 1867. The empire recognized 11 official nationalities within its borders.[1] And in the decades before World War I, many of these groups showed strong support for self-rule and liberty.

The emperor allowed the creation of two separate parliaments: one in Austria and one in Hungary. Even so, the emperor had final say on all matters. In the Hungarian part of the empire, the Parliament largely ignored the demands of people of different nationalities. In the Austrian part of the empire, national minorities were represented in Parliament. While representation in the Austrian government gave these groups a voice, it also created more tension. Few national minorities were united under a single political party. Instead, representatives were members of various nationalist parties. This created a parliament that was very diverse but filled with friction. Despite this turmoil, between 1867 and 1914, the Austrian Parliament managed to pass some reforms giving minority nationalities more rights.

In the two years before World War I, the tension between minority nationalities and the government had reached the boiling point. In early 1914, only five months before World War I broke out, Austria dissolved its national parliament. It remained suspended when Austria-Hungary declared war against Serbia, setting off World War I.

## RUSSIA AND THE ROMANOVS

Though revolution erupted in the Austrian Empire and elsewhere in 1848, it did not take hold in Russia. The czar of Russia had firm control over the country's government and military. But people began challenging this control in the latter half of the 1800s.

In the 1860s, pamphlets began appearing in Saint Petersburg, the capital of Russia. Some called for the creation of an assembly representing the people, while others called for outright revolt against the czarist government. Ten years later, socialism was rising in popularity among Russia's youth. Young people organized public events to rally support for their ideas, which began to take hold in the urban centers where industrial workers toiled.

## THE RULE OF FRANZ JOSEPH I

Franz Joseph became emperor of Austria in 1848 at the age of 18. During his rule, he dealt with increasing demands for an independent Hungary. He remained in power after the dual monarchy of Austria-Hungary was established in 1867. Franz Joseph's son Rudolph was expected to take the aging monarch's place, but Rudolph committed suicide in 1889. This put Franz Joseph's nephew Franz Ferdinand next in line. Franz Joseph ruled until his death in 1916, in the middle of World War I. Since Franz Ferdinand had been assassinated by this time, Franz Joseph's grandnephew Charles I became the new emperor of Austria-Hungary.

In 1894, Nicholas II took the throne. Though he initially took a hard line against reforms, by 1900, Russia had a national assembly that gave the Russian people more of a voice in government. Socialism had also found support among Russian professionals. Meanwhile, Russia suffered defeat in several wars as it attempted to expand its borders. Its focus on imperialism meant it had ignored social reforms at home. People across Russia began organizing and pushing for more power. In January 1905, a group of protesters marched to Nicholas's palace to present their demands. They were met with military gunfire, and approximately 130 protesters were killed.[2]

The czar's actions caused outrage all over Russia. Workers and students organized strikes, and soldiers mutinied. By October 1905, support for revolution had reached a breaking point. Workers across Russia went on strike, bringing cities to a halt. A soviet, or council of elected representatives from a town's factories, was formed in Saint Petersburg. In an effort to quell the revolutionaries, Nicholas allowed the formation of an elected legislature. But protests and mutinies in the military continued for two more years.

Though Nicholas had allowed the establishment of a legislature, the Russian Revolution of 1905 was regarded as a failure. Members of the fledgling Social Democratic Party, based on the philosophy of German thinker Karl Marx, split into two factions. The Mensheviks believed they should work with the new legislature, called the Duma. The Bolsheviks, on the other hand, believed the

Duma was simply a piece of propaganda designed to calm the revolutionaries. Led by Vladimir Lenin, the Bolsheviks would gain popularity throughout World War I and participate in protests that undermined the czar's war effort. In 1917, Lenin and the Bolsheviks led a revolution that overthrew the czar and resulted in Russia's surrender to Germany.

## THE *COMMUNIST MANIFESTO*

In 1848, German philosopher and economist Karl Marx and German social scientist Friedrich Engels wrote the *Communist Manifesto*, a book that was very influential for millions of young Europeans. The *Communist Manifesto* described the unfair economic and social conditions the Hapsburgs and other royal and noble families profited from. It argued for a new society in which all land and goods would be publicly shared and there were no rulers or royalty. The *Communist Manifesto* had a significant impact on many revolutionaries in Europe, including the socialists who led the Russian Revolutions in 1905 and 1917.

## THE OTTOMAN EMPIRE

In the early 1900s, the centuries-old Ottoman Empire was in decline. Between the 1300s and 1600s, the Ottoman Turks had expanded their empire from Turkey into the Balkan Peninsula, the Middle East, North Africa, and present-day Hungary, Greece, and Ukraine. But a series of wars during the 1700s and 1800s had shrunk the Ottoman Empire's territories. By 1900, the Ottoman Empire still controlled much of the Middle East, but its European territories included only a few provinces on the Balkan Peninsula.

In 1905, the Russian military shot at protesters.

As the empire faced defeat on the battlefield, it also faced rising social unrest at home. In the 1860s, a loosely organized secret group of intellectuals called the Young Ottomans formed. The nationalist group wanted to convert the sprawling empire, which including many nationalities, into a single Turkish state. The group also wanted to create a constitutional government. This activity gave rise to another nationalist group, the Young Turks.

The Young Turks were made up of a several smaller nationalist groups within the Ottoman Empire. The Young Turks helped undermine the regime and eventually led a revolution against Ottoman sultan Abdul Hamid II. A group of students in Istanbul, the empire's capital, developed a plan to undermine his regime in 1889, but they were forced to flee to France when their plan was discovered. However, the students continued spreading their ideas for reform and a constitutional government to the people of the Ottoman Empire.

Young Turks within the empire, including those serving in the military, led a revolt against the government in 1908. In response to the revolt, Abdul Hamid established a parliament and constitution. A year later, the Young Turk–led parliament forced Abdul Hamid to resign. The Young Turks cemented their power after the empire lost nearly all its territory in the Balkan Wars in 1912 and 1913, including the provinces of Serbia, Greece, Albania, and Bulgaria. The Young Turks used their power to intimidate the remaining national minorities in the Ottoman Empire in the year before the war. Shortly before World War I broke out, the Ottoman Empire negotiated an alliance with Germany, believing Germany's powerful military would help improve the Ottomans' weak forces.

Abdul Hamid II ruled the Ottoman Empire from 1876 to 1909.

Friedrich Wilhelm IV ruled Prussia from 1840 until his death in 1861.

# GERMANY FLEXES ITS MUSCLES

The 1800s transformed Germany from a group of loosely aligned states to a militaristic, aggressive power with imperial ambitions. Germany's leaders wanted to turn their country into a major player on the world stage. This desire led to diplomatic and military decisions that played a significant role in causing World War I.

In 1848, Germany was a confederation, or political group, made up of several states. These states included Hanover, Bavaria, and, largest of all, Prussia. The confederation did not have a strong central government. By the middle of the 1800s, most of these territories had revolutionaries and freedom fighters demanding change from their leaders. Crop failures in the countryside and a severe depression that eliminated jobs and halted industrial progress in cities prompted civil unrest throughout the confederation.

Reactions to these protests varied throughout the confederation. Some states, such as Frankfurt, passed reforms that expanded the rights of the poor and the working class. Other states took the opposite strategy and suppressed the revolutionaries. The king of Prussia was Friedrich Wilhelm IV, a monarchist who was firmly opposed to any revolution or challenge to royal right of rule. When revolution first broke out in Prussia in March 1848, Friedrich Wilhelm IV brought in the army to stop the revolutionaries. After a series of bloody demonstrations, the king reluctantly gave in. He created a national assembly, only to dissolve it shortly thereafter. In its place, he set up a constitution that gave most of the political power to himself, the military, and government workers.

By the summer of 1849, the revolutions across the confederation had subsided or been crushed. Over the next ten years, the German economy bounced back, and leaders of the major German states took steps to hold on to their power. This started to change in the 1860s. Public opinion turned in favor of unifying the German states as a single nation. This sentiment was no different in the state of Prussia, where the ailing Friedrich Wilhelm IV had been replaced by his brother Wilhelm I. Wilhelm I introduced political reforms that allowed those who supported a more democratic system to be represented in government.

But these reforms were short-lived, as Wilhelm I replaced reformers with advisers and ministers who favored the monarchy. Wilhelm I appointed Otto von Bismarck, the Prussian ambassador to France, as prime minister. Bismarck had a reputation of fighting reforms while supporting a strong military and the monarchy. Bismarck saw the need for cooperation between the reformers and Wilhelm I's regime, but he favored a solution that kept Wilhelm I's political power in place. Bismarck saw that unifying the German states and other political reforms were inevitable, and he

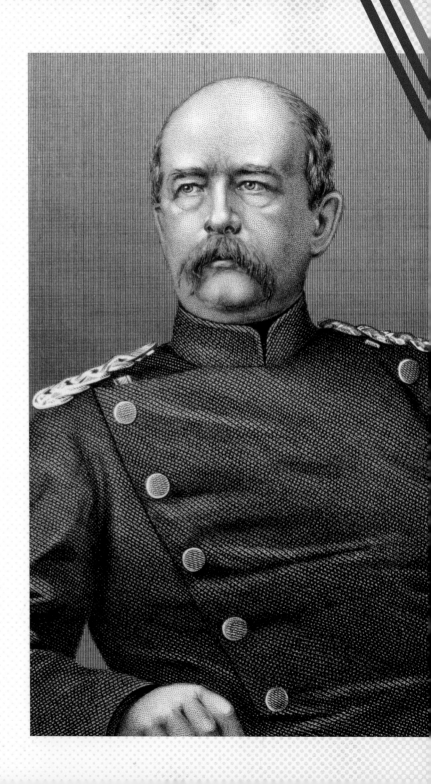

Otto von Bismarck gained the nickname "the Iron Chancellor" because of his powerful style of leadership.

decided to use the military to take an aggressive approach to ensure Wilhelm I's regime remained in power.

Together, Bismarck and Wilhelm I doubled the size of the army and used it to unite many different regions of the German confederation. Under Bismarck's direction, in 1864, the Prussian military invaded Denmark and took land that was predominantly Germanic. Then, Bismarck set his sights on France.

## THE SECOND REICH

In Germany, the period between the unification of Germany and the end of World War I is known as the Second Reich. The First Reich was the long period between 800 and 1806, also known as the Holy Roman Empire. During the Second Reich, Germany experienced rapid economic growth and industrialization, as well as an increase in national pride among Germans. Some Germans developed feelings of superiority over other nations, convinced Germany was destined to become a great world power.

## WAR WITH FRANCE UNITES GERMANY

The Franco-Prussian War began in 1870 as a result of a feud over who the new ruler of Spain should be. The Spanish throne had been vacant since Queen Isabella II was removed in 1868. The Spanish government offered the crown to Prince Leopold of Hohenzollern-Sigmaringen, a Prussian noble. This development worried France because it would mean an alliance between Prussia and Spain, both of which bordered France. French diplomats pressured Prussia to withdraw Leopold's candidacy. But Wilhelm I was unable to promise the French that Leopold would

The German army arrives in Paris during the Franco-Prussian war.

not be considered a candidate in the future. Bismarck released a printed copy of the tense negotiations between himself and the French ambassador, purposely editing the remarks so they were as insulting to the French as possible. He hoped doing so would provoke France into war.

France's emperor, Napoleon III, was furious. He declared war against Prussia on July 19, 1870. The French were confident they could win, but they did not realize a declaration of war would unify southern German states against them. Bismarck's plan was falling into place. Facing a common enemy, the German states and Prussia would unify into a single country. France's attack had provided the excuse Bismarck needed to create a stronger German nation.

The war was short, and France's army was demolished. France officially surrendered on January 28, 1871, after Paris, the capital, had been under siege for months. France lost the territories of Alsace and Lorraine to the new German Empire. This created a rift between France and Germany that would directly lead to their hostility during World War I.

While the Franco-Prussian War left France's military in tatters, the conflict boosted Germans' confidence in the strength of the Prussian military. On January 18, 1871, southern German states united with the large Prussian state to the north under a single banner of power. Wilhelm I was the emperor, and Bismarck was chancellor, or head of the government.

## ALSACE-LORRAINE

The region known as Alsace-Lorraine rests along the border between France and Germany. Long a part of German territory, it was lost to France after the Thirty Years' War in 1631. More than two centuries later, after the Franco-Prussian War, France had to give back the territory. At the time, many people living in Alsace-Lorraine already spoke German. The region boosted Germany's supply of iron-ore, steel-making factories, and other industry. The region would be returned to France after World War I, taken by Germany during World War II (1939–1945), and once again returned to France when the war ended.

## WILHELM II'S BLUSTER AND *WELTPOLITIK*

In 1888, Wilhelm I's grandson Wilhelm II became the head of the German Empire. Two years later, Wilhelm II dismissed Bismarck as chancellor. Though Bismarck had been successful at defeating France and unifying Germany, he had ignored calls for reform within the newly unified nation.

But Wilhelm II did not have a plan of his own for reforming his empire. He was not an effective or diplomatic leader at home or abroad. Anxious to expand Germany's imperial power, Wilhelm II was aggressive in his negotiations with other countries. He was quick to adopt and then abandon dramatic plans for imperial expansion. This behavior made it difficult for other monarchs, and frequently his own advisers, to understand his intentions.

Despite Wilhelm II's blustering over the course of his rule, a foreign policy called *Weltpolitik*, or "world policy," developed.[1] It focused on expanding Germany's influence in the world by competing with the United Kingdom and France for territory and economic power. Instead of forging alliances with other major European powers, Germany would seek diplomatic and trade partners

## GERMANY'S PLACE IN THE SUN

German secretary of state for foreign affairs Bernhard von Bülow described the ambition of *Weltpolitik* in 1897. He said, "The times when the German left the earth to one of his neighbors, the sea to the other, and reserved for himself the heavens where pure philosophy reigns—these times are over. . . . We don't want to put anyone in the shadow, but we too demand our place in the sun."[2]

elsewhere. *Weltpolitik* was popular among the German people, who had become increasingly national minded and militaristic.

Though Germany shied away from building alliances with other European powers, it did plan for military conflict with them. In 1905, German chief of general staff Alfred Graf von Schlieffen developed a strategy in case Germany had to fight a two-front war with France to the west and Russia to the east. The Schlieffen Plan called for Germany to divide its military into two forces, one large and one small. Germany assumed Russia would take longer to mobilize, so the small force would be sent to the east to keep Russia in check. Meanwhile, the large force would be sent west to defeat France in a single, massive attack. The larger force would then move east, join the smaller force, and defeat Russia.

Germany's history of military strength, its arrogant emperor, and the nationalistic German public helped create a nation aggressively intent on expanding its influence in Europe, even if that meant going to war with its neighbors.

# KAISER WILHELM II

## 1859–1941

Kaiser Wilhelm II was emperor of Germany from 1888 until the end of World War I. He was born in 1859 to Germany's Frederick III and Victoria, who was the oldest daughter of Queen Victoria of England. Wilhelm II was born with a withered arm, which some historians have said helped make him an unpleasant and disagreeable person. Wilhelm II's grandfather Wilhelm I died in 1888. Wilhelm I's son Frederick III was meant to be the next emperor but ruled for only 99 days; he died of throat cancer not long after his coronation.

As kaiser, Wilhelm II increased military power and forced chancellor Otto von Bismarck to resign in 1890. In an interview with the British newspaper the *Daily Telegraph* in 1908, Wilhelm II made a number of insulting political statements against the United Kingdom, France, and Russia. For example, he said English people were "mad, mad, mad as March hares."[3] These comments helped fan the flames of war.

The Crimean War was one example of European powers attempting to expand their empires in the 1800s.

# CHAPTER ★ 4 ★

# THE LAST BREATH OF EUROPEAN IMPERIALISM

While Europe's major powers dealt with demands for more rights and freedoms, they continued competing with each other to expand their empires. They did so with a mix of military action and diplomacy. Between 1853 and 1914, a series of wars shifted the borders between European nations. These conflicts created enemies and allies that would define the opposing sides in World War I.

By the mid-1800s, the Ottoman Empire was in decline. Russia, home to many Slavs, shared cultural ties with Serbia and other Balkan provinces. Russia was also eager to expand its influence in the region surrounding the Black Sea, where the Ottoman Empire had control. In 1853, Russia initiated the Crimean War, hoping to conquer territory in the region.

Threatened by the idea of an expanded Russian empire, the United Kingdom and France joined the conflict on the side of the Ottomans. The United Kingdom was anxious to maintain its own empire by securing trade with the Ottomans. France was desperate for military glory and wanted revenge for its defeat by Russia in the Napoleonic Wars in the early 1800s.

Most of the battles were fought on the Crimean Peninsula, which lies between the Black Sea and the Sea of Azov. After three years of fighting, the Russians lost the war. They gave up territory and were no longer allowed to have military or trading ships along the Black Sea. Each side lost approximately 250,000 soldiers, many due to causes unrelated to combat, such as disease.[1] The immediate result of this war was that the Ottomans were free from

## THE LIGHT BRIGADE

During the Crimean War, one of the British cavalry units was known as the Light Brigade. On October 25, 1854, the unit's leader misinterpreted an order and led his brigade of approximately 670 troops into a valley heavily defended by Russian troops.[2] The British troops were slaughtered as they charged into the valley. The Light Brigade suffered major losses, but it maintained order in the valley and was able to briefly disorganize the Russians. The story of the Light Brigade became very popular with the British public. Alfred, Lord Tennyson, a British poet, wrote a poem called "The Charge of the Light Brigade," which includes the line, "Into the valley of Death/Rode the six hundred."[3]

Russian pressure. However, the conflict did little to put an end to the tensions within the region, and it did not dissuade other European powers from trying to stake their own claims.

## CONFLICT CONTINUES

The Balkan states continued to suffer under Ottoman rule after the Crimean War. The period between 1876 and 1878, in particular, was a time of conflict between European nations and the Ottomans.

Serbia and Montenegro, two self-governing provinces in the Ottoman Empire, both declared war on the Ottoman Empire in 1876 and proclaimed full independence. These wars were called the Serbian-Ottoman War and the Montenegrin-Ottoman War, respectively. Many Russian volunteers who believed in the Slavic cause joined the war on the side of Serbia and Montenegro. In 1877, Russia declared war on the Ottoman Empire as well. This was known as the Russo-Turkish War.

This time, Russia was successful. With help from Serbians and Montenegrins, Russia defeated the Ottomans in 1878. The conflict formally ended with the Treaty of San Stefano on March 3, 1878. The treaty made Serbia and Montenegro fully independent countries. In addition, Bulgaria became a self-governing province within the Russian Empire. The regions of Bosnia and Herzegovina remained in the Ottoman Empire but became self-governing. The agreement nearly eliminated the Ottoman Empire's European territory.

Russia's success was short-lived, however. The terms of the Treaty of San Stefano created panic in other European empires, especially Austria-Hungary and the United Kingdom. Austria-Hungary, as the Balkan Peninsula's neighbor to the west, feared the creation of independent Slavic nations would weaken Austria-Hungary's influence in the region. Leaders in the United Kingdom believed the treaty gave too much influence to Russia, especially in the creation of Bulgaria.

In the spring of 1878, leaders of the major powers, including Russia, the United Kingdom, and Austria-Hungary, met in Berlin, Germany, to modify the Treaty of San Stefano. The Treaty of Berlin maintained the independent status of Serbia and Montenegro. However, the treaty made Bulgaria much smaller and turned it into a self-governing state that was technically part of the Ottoman Empire. This agreement reversed many of the gains Russia had made in the Russo-Turkish War.

According to the Treaty of Berlin, Bosnia and Herzegovina were still technically part of the Ottoman Empire. In reality, however, these provinces were occupied by the Austro-Hungarian military. The treaty failed to address the demands of the Balkan peoples, setting the stage for future conflict on the peninsula.

Russian troops, wearing gray, defeated Ottoman troops in an 1877 battle during the Russo-Turkish War.

## MORE TROUBLE FOR RUSSIA

After suffering humiliation in the Balkans at the hands of its European rivals, Russia turned its attention to expanding its influence in Asia. It hoped to gain territory on the Korean Peninsula and the Chinese region of Manchuria. After

Russian and Turkish leaders sign the Treaty of San Stefano in 1878.

issuing warnings to Russia to remove its troops from the region, Japan declared war in 1904.

Russia had a difficult time getting troops and supplies across its vast territory to the conflict in the Far East. A year later, Japan and Russia negotiated a peace that stripped Russia of its modest territory in Manchuria and gave control of the

Korean Peninsula to Japan. The war cost thousands of Russian lives and took a toll on the Russian economy, leading to unrest at home.

## ANOTHER BLOW TO THE OTTOMAN EMPIRE

The Ottoman Empire continued to see a decline in its territory, power, and influence. In 1911, Italy declared war against the Ottomans to expand its power in North Africa. Italian forces invaded the Ottoman provinces of Tripolitania and Cyrenaica in modern Libya.

Italy was able to quickly overtake and control these provinces, revealing how militarily weak the Ottoman Empire had become. In 1912, the Ottomans gave up control of Tripolitania and Cyrenaica to Italy as they faced yet another military conflict in the Balkan Peninsula.

## GERMANY JOINS LATE IN THE GAME

After the unification of Germany in 1871, Chancellor Bismarck focused the country's foreign policy on maintaining Germany's borders and security rather than expanding

### THE TRANS-SIBERIAN RAILWAY

Russia's job of getting troops and supplies to the front lines in the Russo-Japanese War was made slightly easier thanks to the Trans-Siberian Railway. Started in 1891 and completed in 1904, the railroad connected the western city of Moscow to the eastern city of Vladivostok, a stretch of more than 5,000 miles (8,000 km).[4] The original route ran through the Chinese territory of Manchuria. However, following its loss to Japan, Russia worried Japan would take over Manchuria and have access to the railway. In 1916, Russia completed a longer stretch that bypassed Manchuria. The Trans-Siberian Railway helped bring industrialization to the vast Russian region of Siberia.

Japanese soldiers defeated Russian forces at the battle of Yalu River during the Russo-Japanese War.

them. But Wilhelm II hoped to increase Germany's territory and influence in Europe, Africa, and Asia. He replaced Bismarck as chancellor with Leo von Caprivi, who added 150,000 troops to the German army and doubled spending on the military.[5] Germany then attempted to gain colonies in Africa. This action displeased the United Kingdom, which had a number of colonies in Africa and saw Germany's move into the region as a threat to its own empire. Anglo-German relations became more stressed when Wilhelm II announced plans to build up the German navy. Historically, the United Kingdom had been the world's dominant naval power.

## COLONIAL STAKES IN AFRICA

Few countries in Africa were independent at the outbreak of World War I. Most were carved into colonies by European imperial powers. France controlled most of West Africa, including present-day Algeria, Morocco, Senegal, Mauritania, Mali, and Niger. The United Kingdom held territory in East Africa, including present-day Egypt and Sudan, as well as present-day South Africa, Botswana, Zimbabwe, and Zambia. Germany, Italy, Portugal, Spain, and Belgium also had colonial stakes in Africa.

In an effort to compete with the United Kingdom and France for colonies in Africa, Germany started a campaign to expand its influence in the North African territory of Morocco. In 1904, France and Spain agreed to divide control of Morocco between themselves. Such an agreement threatened German interests in the region. Wilhelm II spoke out against the agreement, stating Morocco had the right to be independent. The declaration started a flurry of talks that resulted in upholding Germany's economic interest in Morocco while allowing France and Spain to police the region.

In 1911, Wilhelm II made another move to anger the French. He sent a German gunboat to patrol the sea along the Moroccan coast, supposedly to protect German interests during a rebellion there. The bold move set off an

## A VAST EMPIRE

There is a saying that at the height of its power, the sun never set on the British Empire. The nation had lands all over the globe, from India in the east, Canada in the west, Australia and South Africa to the south, and various colonies in between. The empire expanded its reach through military conquest, trade, and missionary work. Due to the British Empire's vast size, many of its territories had some degree of self-rule. World War I played a role in moving these territories toward independence.

international crisis, and the United Kingdom even took steps to prepare for war with Germany. Negotiations helped the nations avoid military conflict and gave Germany territory in the French Congo. However, the events strengthened the United Kingdom's ties with France and its distrust of Germany, further forming the sides that would take shape in World War I.

## SPLENDID ISOLATION

Despite the United Kingdom's success in the Crimean War, the country turned its attention away from expanding its empire in the latter decades of the 1800s. Instead, it focused on maintaining its vast territory. The United Kingdom tended to avoid military conflicts with other European nations. Even so, it kept an interest in maintaining alliances.

By 1900, however, the United Kingdom's policy of "splendid isolation" had run its course.[6] The British Empire was facing challenges to its imperial superiority from Germany, Russia, and France. It became increasingly interested in the outcomes of the military conflicts between Germany, Russia, Austria-Hungary, and the Ottoman Empire, and it took steps to make alliances that would secure its interests in the Balkans and the Middle East. As had the military conflicts of the late 1800s and the crisis in Morocco in 1911, these alliances helped define the fighting sides in the Great War to come.

British prime minister Benjamin Disraeli was one of the main supporters of the "splendid isolation" policy.

Miles Obilic leads a charge during the battle of Kosovo in 1389.

# TROUBLE IN THE BALKANS

By 1900, the people living in the Balkan Peninsula had been under near-continuous foreign rule for more than 500 years. In the 1800s, the region saw an increase in political and military conflicts, as empires such as Russia and Austria-Hungary showed renewed interest in the territories. These conflicts caused the region to become unstable, creating tensions that would soon lead to a global war.

June 28, the date of Archduke Franz Ferdinand's assassination in 1914, was of special significance for Slavs. On that date in 1389, a Serbian army lost to the Ottoman Turks in the battle of Kosovo.

That loss led to the occupation of Slavic lands for the next 300 years. But the Turks could not crush the spirit of Serbian rebellion. By the 1600s, a series of weak rulers had forced the Ottoman Empire into decline. Ottoman soldiers, who were fighting to maintain Turkish control along the empire's borders, moved inward as the empire lost territory to its rivals. As the Ottoman soldiers moved, they were met with resistance from the Slavs living there. In 1690, Serbs living in the northern part of the empire gave armed support to a force of invading Austrians. Serbs did the same thing nearly 100 years later when war broke out between the Ottoman Empire on one side and Austria-Hungary and its ally Russia on the other.

The Ottomans' war with Austria-Hungary and Russia ended in two treaties that were supposed to give Serbs in the empire more rights. However, the Ottomans failed to make good on this part of the treaty. This created unrest in Serbia, which was still under Ottoman control. With support from both Russia and Austria, Serbia rose up in rebellion against the Ottomans in 1804. After more than a decade of war against the

## MILOS OBILIC, NATIONAL HERO

The 1389 battle of Kosovo was an important chapter in the history of Serbia. One particular story made it into the country's folklore. Early in the battle, a Serbian noble named Milos Obilic snuck into the camp of the Turkish sultan, Murad I. Pretending to be a deserter, Obilic made it to the sultan's tent and stabbed him with a poison-tipped dagger. Though the Serbs suffered defeat in the battle of Kosovo, Obilic is considered a national hero.

Ottomans, Serbia finally gained some right to self-rule, including the right to organize its own local assembly.

## ANNEXATION LEADS TO WAR

Following the Treaty of Berlin in 1878, Austria-Hungary was in control of Bosnia and Herzegovina, even though these provinces were technically still part of the Ottoman Empire. At this time, nearly 40 percent of the population in Bosnia and Herzegovina was Serbs.[1] Austria-Hungary, as the occupying force, swiftly crushed any signs of nationalism in these provinces. Austria-Hungary also suppressed circulation of newspapers from neighboring independent Serbia and disbanded some Serbian cultural groups. But Austria-Hungary also improved the efficiency of Bosnia and Herzegovina's industry and agriculture, which in turn gave an economic boost to people living there.

Despite its modest domestic gains in the provinces, Austria-Hungary continued to be extremely wary of the influence Serbia had in Bosnia and Herzegovina. Austria-Hungary's occupation of Bosnia-Herzegovina was set to expire in 1908, at which point it had every intention of annexing the provinces into its empire, a move that was sure to anger Serbia and Serb nationals throughout the region.

On October 5, 1908, Austria-Hungary announced its annexation of Bosnia and Herzegovina, immediately throwing Europe into turmoil. Austria-Hungary's move outraged Serbia and its ally Russia, prompting the threat of military intervention. The move also destroyed any chance of cooperation between Russia and Austria-Hungary when crises arose in the Balkan Peninsula. In addition, the annexation seemed to close the door on Russia's imperial ambitions in the region.

## THE BALKAN WARS

Italy's successful invasion of Ottoman territory in North Africa in 1911 set the stage for a rebellion against Ottoman rule in the Balkans. In 11 months, Italy had successfully taken the provinces of Cyrenaica and Tripolitania from Ottoman control, exposing the declining empire's weakness. While Italy's triumph in the Italo-Turkish War (1911–1912) strengthened its own imperial power, the victory destabilized the balance of power between Italy's neighbors, particularly in the Balkan Peninsula.

Before the Italo-Turkish War was even finished, states in the Balkan Peninsula were already organizing against the Ottoman Empire. With help from Russia, the countries of Serbia, Bulgaria, Greece, and Montenegro formed the Balkan League with the intent to take control of Macedonia from the Ottomans. Macedonia declared war on the Ottoman Empire on October 8, 1912, ten days before the Ottomans' war with Italy ended. The Balkan League joined the fight in

Italian soldiers fire at Ottoman forces in a 1912 battle during the Italo-Turkish War.

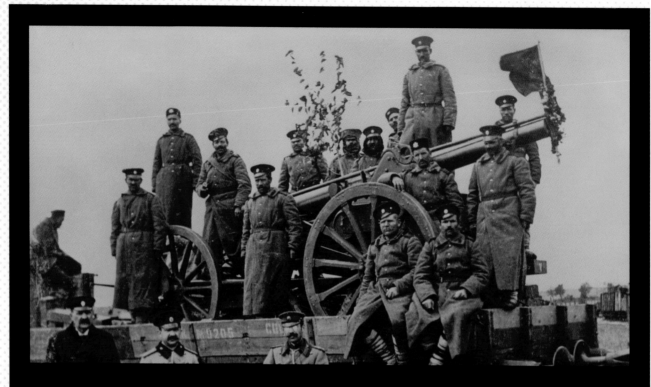

Bulgarian soldiers pose with a cannon they captured during the First Balkan War.

the First Balkan War (1912–1913) on the day the Ottomans signed a peace treaty with Italy.

With Ottoman troops deployed in North Africa, Macedonia and the Balkan League achieved a swift victory. In less than two months a truce was declared, but fighting resumed after the Young Turks staged a coup, taking over the nearly defunct Ottoman Empire. The Balkan League was victorious once again, and a peace treaty was signed in May 1913. The Ottoman Empire had lost all of its European territory.

Just one month later, disagreements between Bulgaria and Serbia and their Greek and Romanian allies over how to divide Macedonia turned violent. The Second Balkan War (1913) lasted only three months. At the end, Greece and Serbia received most of Macedonia. Left largely without spoils, Bulgaria turned to Austria-Hungary, Serbia's enemy, for help. Meanwhile, Serbia found a friend in Russia. With major European powers—and by extension their allies—choosing sides in the Balkans, the stage was set for the unstable region to erupt into war.

## BULGARIA AT WAR

After losing to Serbia in the Second Balkan War, the kingdom of Bulgaria sided with Serbia's enemies, Germany and Austria-Hungary, in World War I. Bulgaria declared war on Serbia on October 1, 1915. Bulgaria invaded Macedonia to cut off Serbia from the aid of its allies. Neighboring Greece was a neutral country in the early stages of World War I, and it gave up land to the Bulgarians in order to maintain neutrality. Despite this, Bulgaria launched an offensive against Greece in August 1916. The offensive went well at first, but British aerial bombs eventually drove the Bulgarians back. Bulgaria signed an armistice with British and Greek forces on September 29, 1918. By the end of September, Bulgaria was forced to sign a treaty that dramatically reduced the size of its army.

The German army marched into neutral Belgium in 1914. This act prompted the United

# DUELING ALLIANCES

In the decades leading to World War I, an increasingly complex system of alliances shaped the relations between European powers. While these alliances did not directly cause the war, the major powers' diplomatic efforts created a system that required nations to go to war to defend or support their allies.

In 1839, leaders from across Europe met to discuss an agreement that became known as the Treaty of London. According to the agreement, the United Kingdom was required to defend the neutrality of Belgium, a country that lay between France and the German confederation. If another country invaded Belgium, the United Kingdom had to come to Belgium's aid.

The treaty would stand until the beginning of World War I, and it played a key role in bringing the United Kingdom into the conflict. After declaring war on France on August 3, 1914, Germany hoped to march through Belgium as a shortcut to Paris. The Germans asked the United Kingdom to ignore its promise to Belgium, but the British denied this request.

## THE DUAL ALLIANCE BECOMES THE TRIPLE ALLIANCE

In 1879, Austria-Hungary and Germany signed the Dual Alliance, an agreement to support each other if either one was attacked by Russia. The alliance was a strategy of mutual support. It also specified that if one of them were attacked by another power, the other would remain neutral. Bismarck was the German chancellor in 1879. He believed the alliance would deter Russia from attacking Germany, as Russia would be reluctant to attack both Germany and Austria-Hungary at once.

Italy joined the pact in 1882, turning the Dual Alliance into the Triple Alliance. The pact's terms changed slightly to accommodate the addition, but mutual support was still the focus. Italy's

### NEUTRALITY

Many agreements between European powers relied on the concept of neutrality. When a country agreed to be neutral, it agreed not to help or in any way support another nation at war. Under the terms of an 1887 treaty, Germany had to remain neutral if Russia went to war with another country. Germany did not have to help Russia, but according to the treaty, it could not help or support Russia's enemy either. Neutrality also played a role in the Great War. Belgium, Italy, and the United States were neutral at the outbreak of World War I. However, circumstances eventually led them all to choose sides.

German and Austro-Hungarian leaders meet to discuss the Dual Alliance in 1879.

concern was aggression from France, not Russia. If France attacked Italy, Austria-Hungary and Germany would come to Italy's aid. In return, Italy would remain neutral in a conflict between Austria-Hungary and Russia.

However, the relationship between Italy and Austria-Hungary became increasingly strained in the years leading up to World War I because of territorial disputes in the northern Adriatic and the Balkan Peninsula. Though Italy would renew its alliance with Germany and Austria-Hungary three times before World War I, it also pursued a secret alliance with France at the same time. By 1915, the relationship between Italy and Austria-Hungary had broken down to the point that Italy joined the war on the side of France.

## THE RACCONIGI BARGAIN

In 1909, Italy once again broke its promise to the Triple Alliance. It signed a secret agreement with Russia called the Racconigi Bargain. It stated that Italy or Russia had to consult the other before either came to any agreements with other nations regarding the Balkans. Russia had to accept Italy's interests in North Africa, while Italy did the same with Russia's interests in the Balkan Peninsula. However, Italy would invalidate this agreement by signing yet another secret agreement with Austria-Hungary.

## GERMANY AND RUSSIA'S REINSURANCE TREATY

While Germany was allied with Austria-Hungary and Italy, it came to an agreement with Russia in 1887. Chancellor Bismarck was the mastermind of this agreement, known as the Reinsurance Treaty. It required Germany and Russia to remain neutral in the event that either of them were at war with a third-party nation. However, there were two notable exceptions to this rule. Due to preexisting alliances, the treaty would not apply if Russia attacked Austria-Hungary or if Germany attacked France.

The Reinsurance Treaty was not popular at home in Germany. In the years prior to 1887, the Russian press had taken an aggressive tone against Germany.

Many Russians believed Russia had the right to protect the Slavic states in the Balkans. They thought Germany, as an ally of Austria-Hungary, would try to promote Austria-Hungary's agenda in the region. These sentiments made many Germans skeptical that the Reinsurance Treaty would actually protect Germany from Russian aggression in the event of war with a third power. Though it protected Germany from fighting a two-front war if France attacked the empire, the Reinsurance Treaty was not renewed in 1890. This left Russia free to pursue alliances elsewhere.

## FRANCO-RUSSIAN ALLIANCE

After the Reinsurance Treaty was not renewed, Russia sought a diplomatic relationship with France. By 1894, the two countries were friendly enough to come to a secret agreement. The Franco-Russian Alliance stated that if France was invaded by Germany or Germany's ally Italy, Russia would send nearly one million troops to help defend France. Likewise, if Russia was invaded by Germany or by Germany's ally Austria-Hungary, France would send 1.3 million men to defend Russia.[1]

The Franco-Russian Alliance was renewed in 1899 and again in 1912. The alliance between France and Russia left Germany vulnerable to a two-front war—exactly what Bismarck had attempted to avoid.

## FRANCO-ITALIAN ENTENTE

Three years after France renewed its alliance with Russia in 1899, it entered into another defensive agreement of mutual support, this time with Italy. France and Italy agreed to remain neutral if either entered into a war with a third power. Additionally, France would recognize Italy's interests in Libya, while Italy would do the same for France in Morocco.

Entering into an alliance with France seemed counterproductive for Italy, which was allied with Germany and Austria-Hungary in part to protect it from aggression from France. However, the Italians had become increasingly skeptical that their interests lay in an alliance

**A French newspaper published this illustration depicting the Franco-Russian Alliance in 1897.**

with Germany and Austria-Hungary. Many Italians believed Austria-Hungary's actions in the Balkans conflicted with Italian interests in the region. An alliance with France helped Italy strengthen its defenses against other nations while avoiding conflicts of interest with Austria-Hungary.

## ENTENTE CORDIALE

By 1904, it became clear to the leaders of the United Kingdom that the empire's policy of isolation would not adequately defend its imperial interests. Other nations had caught up to the United Kingdom in terms of technology and military forces, and they were challenging the empire's naval might and global reach.

## WHAT'S THE DIFFERENCE?

While an alliance, an entente, and a treaty are all types of diplomatic agreements, each type of agreement is slightly different. An entente, such as the one between France and the United Kingdom or the United Kingdom and Russia, is the most informal agreement. It is a friendly understanding between two countries, but it does not require those countries to support each other militarily. An alliance, such as the Dual Alliance between Germany and Austria-Hungary, is a more formal agreement. It outlines obligations between countries that are mutually beneficial. A treaty is the most formal agreement. Countries draft a treaty together, and then the government of each nation must sign it for it to go into effect.

Though France and the United Kingdom had been imperial rivals, each saw the value in putting aside their differences. France believed a diplomatic friendship with the United Kingdom would be another check on German aggression. Both saw how such an agreement would benefit them in their

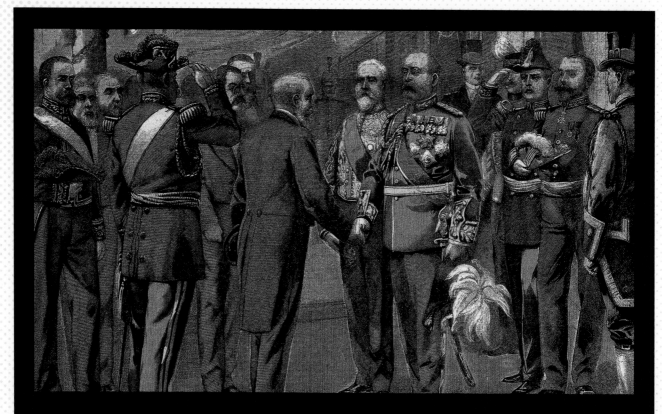

The president of France greets the king of the United Kingdom, *right*, prior to the signing of the Entente Cordiale.

dealings with their African colonies. The entente specified that the United Kingdom was free to act in Egypt without French interference; similarly, France could act in Morocco without British intervention. Though the agreement, known as the Entente Cordiale, did not require either nation to come to the other's defense, it laid the foundation for an alliance when World War I broke out.

## ANGLO-RUSSIAN ENTENTE

The United Kingdom continued to expand its diplomatic relationships in 1907, when it came to an agreement with Russia. Russia and the United Kingdom both had imperial interests in Asia. Coming to an agreement would make diplomacy between the countries more stable. The entente outlined each country's interests in Persia (now Iran) and the United Kingdom's interest in Afghanistan. It also required both countries to stay out of Tibet's domestic affairs.

Similar to the entente with France, the Anglo-Russian Entente paved the way for the United Kingdom's alliance with Russia in World War I. Indeed, in 1907, Russia, the United Kingdom, and France entered into the Triple Entente. The agreement stated that the nations were morally obligated to support each other.

By 1907, the major powers' hands were tied. If war broke out between just two nations, their tangle of alliances ensured everyone else would be pulled into the conflict. When Austria-Hungary declared war on Serbia in July 1914, that is exactly what happened.

## ANGLO-JAPANESE ALLIANCE

The United Kingdom signed the Anglo-Japanese Alliance with Japan in 1902. The agreement of mutual support attempted to curb Russian expansion in China and Korea. The Anglo-Japanese Alliance was renewed in 1905 and 1911, and it lasted through World War I.

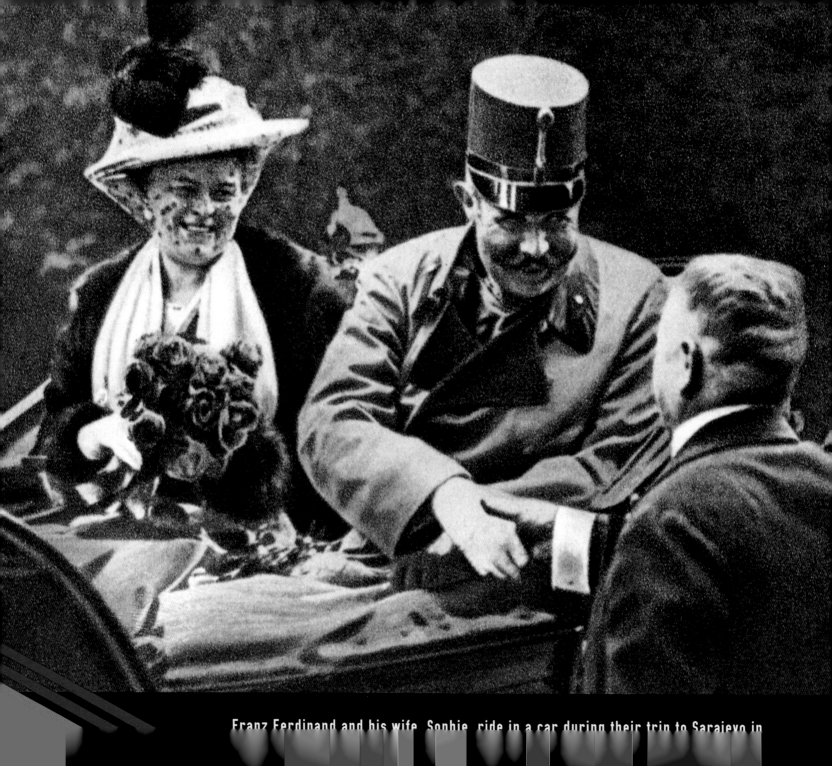

Franz Ferdinand and his wife, Sophie, ride in a car during their trip to Sarajevo in

# A CONSPIRACY LEADS TO ASSASSINATION

Assassination attempts on men with power were common in the early 1900s. Between 1886 and the beginning of World War I, there were more than 40 assassination attempts made on government officials throughout Europe and Asia.[1] Russia, Germany, Austria-Hungary, and other countries could no longer keep revolution from boiling over.

The Slavs in the Balkans never forgot how they were forced from one oppressive regime (the Ottomans) to another (the Austro-Hungarians) without ever having a say in the creation of an independent Slavic state. Slavs in Serbia were overwhelmingly opposed to Austro-Hungarian rule.

The Austro-Hungarian government was quick to outlaw student demonstrations, jail agitators calling for Slavic independence, and deny the very idea of Slavic freedom. But this government suppression backfired. Austro-Hungarian opposition made Croats, Serbs, and Slovenians more unified than ever.

At the head of the opposition were young college students. Universities were a relatively recent phenomenon in the Balkan region in the early 1900s; only major cities had them. These places became hubs for radical student organizations and terrorist groups, especially those fighting for Slavic freedom. Most of these students were extremely poor, often sons of serfs or peasants. Many considered themselves socialists. The students had to meet in secret, as they would be imprisoned or even executed if they were caught with anti-Austrian or prorevolutionary literature. A group known as Young Bosnia was born from these secret meetings.

## AN OPPORTUNITY FOR ASSASSINATION

In early 1914, the news came that Franz Ferdinand would be visiting Sarajevo to oversee military maneuvers. A local newspaper had printed the archduke's route through the Sarajevo streets months in advance of his trip. Many Young Bosnia members saw this newspaper article as an opportunity for assassination.

A Young Bosnian cut out the newspaper clipping and mailed it to his friend Nedeljko Cabrinovic. The newspaper clipping Cabrinovic received was unaccompanied by any note or letter, as all Bosnians knew Austro-Hungarian authorities would be monitoring the mail. The only safe way to communicate through mail was by code. After receiving the clipping, Cabrinovic showed it to his friend Gavrilo Princip, a 19-year-old son of a shepherd. Princip, who had dreams of becoming a poet, had joined Young Bosnia in 1911.

## ASSASSINS RECRUITED

Princip and Cabrinovic discovered they had the same idea. Princip was the first to ask if his friend would be willing to join a plot to assassinate Franz Ferdinand. Cabrinovic agreed. Next, they invited a third conspirator, Trifko Grabez. Grabez was the 18-year-old son of an Orthodox priest, and he had recently been kicked out of school for hitting a teacher.

## TYRANNICIDE

Tyrannicide is another name for the killing of a leader. It is one of the oldest methods of inciting revolution. When Franz Ferdinand's assassins were on trial, they invoked the ancient law of tyrannicide in defense of their actions. One of the most notable instances of tyrannicide in history is when Roman emperor Julius Caesar was murdered by his friend Brutus, who feared Caesar was a dictator who would take over the senate. When John Wilkes Booth assassinated American president Abraham Lincoln in 1865, Booth viewed his act as tyrannicide.

Princip contacted his friend Danilo Ilic, asking if Ilic could recruit more assassins. Ilic would ultimately be in charge of both recruiting and organizing the assassination. Princip already had three assassins: himself, Cabrinovic, and Grabez. Ilic recruited three more. The first was Cvjetko Popovic, a Bosnian student who did not start out as a radical revolutionary but became one after spending four months in jail under accusations of radicalism. The second was Vaso Cubrilovic, a Young Bosnian student whose brother Veljko was also convicted as part of the assassination plot for helping hide the weapons. The third was Muhamed Mehmedbasic, a cabinetmaker.

None of these men were highly trained assassins; they were not even competent with guns. Ilic's idea was that even if one assassin lost his nerve or missed his target, it would be extremely unlikely for all of them to miss.

A group known as the Black Hand supplied Young Bosnia's weapons. Both Young Bosnia and the Black Hand aimed for the liberation of Slavs but approached their goals from completely different political sides. Young Bosnia was a radical left-wing student group that believed in freedom, open societies, and abolishing royal rule. The Black Hand was a right-wing military organization secretly headed by members of Serbian military intelligence. Its members believed in violent military conquest and a strong army dictatorship. Most of the Black Hand's members were part of the Serbian military and dreamed of overthrowing their government. They viewed Serbia's leader, King Petar, as too

Two years before the assassination, Princip was kicked out of school for taking part in protests against the Austro-Hungarian government.

weak and moderate. Young Bosnia's vision of a free and open society may have been different from the Black Hand's dream of military dominance. But both groups wanted freedom for Slavs, and that common goal was enough for them to join forces.

The assassins managed to contact the Black Hand through a Bosnian friend. Neither they nor the Austro-Hungarian government knew about the many Black Hand members in the highest levels of the Serbian military. The leader of the Black Hand was Colonel Dragutin Dimitrijevic, also known by the code name Apis. He was a gifted military leader and privately concerned with the Slavic cause. This made him a natural ally with Young Bosnia, even though his political views were very different.

Apis supplied Princip, Cabrinovic, and Grabez with weapons in Belgrade, Serbia. He gave them four pistols and six bombs, as well as poison for each of them to take in case they were captured. Now the three men had to travel 200 miles (320 km) to Sarajevo and sneak across the border carrying pistols, ammunition, poison, and at least one small bomb each.[2]

## JUNE 28, 1914

Franz Ferdinand and his wife would travel through the Appel Quay, a narrow street in Sarajevo, on June 28, 1914. Their destination was the town hall at the end of the road. To Franz Ferdinand's security men, this seemed like the safest street to take. On one side were Austrian-built houses and shops. On the other side of the street was the Miljacka River. Traveling next to a river would make it more difficult for assassins to attack from that side. During the trip, there were

# DRAGUTIN DIMITRIJEVIC

## 1876–1917

Dragutin Dimitrijevic was born in Belgrade, Serbia, and joined a military academy when he was 16. After graduating, he became an officer in the Serbian army. In 1903, at the age of 26, Dimitrijevic led a group of military officers in the assassination of Serbia's king. He later became a professor at the military academy, and his planning helped Serbia during the Balkan Wars of the early 1910s. Dimitrijevic's code name, Apis, referred to a god from Egyptian mythology.

Dimitrijevic was determined to achieve independence for all Slavs in the Balkans. In 1911, he sent a man to assassinate Emperor Franz Joseph, but the attempt failed. Dimitrijevic became the head of Serbian intelligence and the secret leader of a pro-Slavic terrorist organization called the Black Hand. From these positions of power, Dimitrijevic helped arm Franz Ferdinand's assassins and orchestrated their smuggling into Bosnia.

Dimitrijevic was arrested in 1917 after the Austrian government cracked down on Black Hand members and his role in the plot was revealed. He was shot at sunrise on June 24, 1917.

Princip, *right*, sits with two fellow conspirators shortly before leaving for Sarajevo.

three bridges Franz Ferdinand would have to go past on the way to the town hall: the Cumurija Bridge, the Latin Bridge, and the Kaiser Bridge.

A team of special detectives traveled in the front of the motorcade. The mayor of Sarajevo and chief of police rode in the second car, and Franz Ferdinand and Sophie rode in the third car. The fourth and fifth cars carried members of Franz Ferdinand's staff. Meanwhile, not far from the intersection of the Appel Quay and the Latin Bridge, Danilo Ilic was pacing nervously. He was overseeing the operation from the first bridge, and even with the assassins placed and ready, he still had his doubts. Local police did not notice how suspicious he looked, nor did they notice the large coats the other assassins were wearing to cover the bombs hanging from their belts.

Mehmedbasic, Cabrinovic, Cubrilovic, and Popovic stood by the Cumurja Bridge, in front of a police station. Ilic and Princip stood on opposite sides of the Latin Bridge. Finally, Grabez stood along the Kaiser Bridge, the last hope in case Franz Ferdinand managed to escape the other assassins.

## THE FIRST ATTEMPT

The first four assassins saw the motorcade arriving. Mehmedbasic was first up. Just as he had lost his nerve in a previous assassination attempt, he lost his nerve again. Later, when he was being interrogated, Mehmedbasic said he did not throw the bomb because a policeman was right behind him.

Next up was Cubrilovic. The archduke passed by, and Cubrilovic also did nothing. His reason was that he did not know Franz Ferdinand's wife would be next to the archduke, and he worried about hurting an innocent woman.

Then it was Popovic's turn, but he failed as well. "I had no courage," he said at his trial. "I do not know what happened to me."[3]

Cabrinovic was next. He turned to a local policeman standing nearby and asked, "In which car is his Majesty?"[4] The policeman replied the archduke was in the third car. Cabrinovic took the bomb out from under his jacket and threw it. Cabrinovic miscounted, however, and the bomb went off a bit too late, underneath the wheels of the fourth car—behind Franz Ferdinand and his wife.

As people panicked, Cabrinovic quickly swallowed his poison and leaped into the Miljacka River, a dive of 26 feet (8 m). Cabrinovic was surprised to survive not only the fall but also the poison, which was expired and no longer effective. The police were waiting for him as he swam to shore. Before taking him away, the police asked who he was and he said, "I am a Serb hero."[5]

The explosion underneath the fourth car had not killed anyone, although two officers were injured by bomb fragments and sent to the hospital. Franz Ferdinand was furious.

Princip heard the explosion but did not know whether it had succeeded or failed. He saw Cabrinovic being led away by police. He learned the attack had not been successful, and he immediately moved to his backup plan: find another assassination point along the motorcade's return route.

Once Franz Ferdinand was assured no one was seriously harmed, the rest of the motorcade continued up to the town hall without incident. The party went inside the town hall and planned an alternate escape route. The archduke wanted to go to the hospital and visit the men injured by the first bomb. He continued

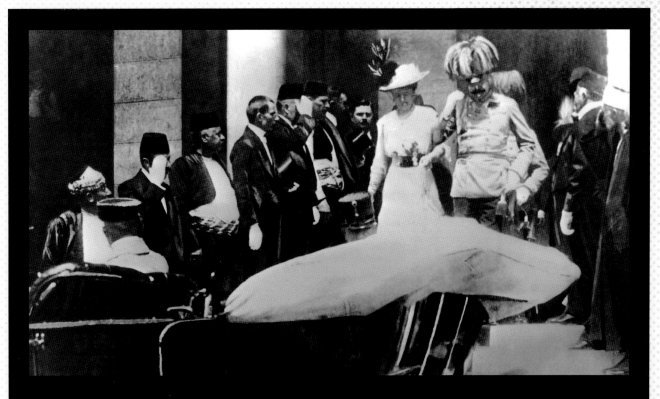

Franz Ferdinand and his wife prepare to get into their car minutes before the assassination.

ranting and insulting those around him. He tried to get Sophie to leave, but she pledged to not leave his side and offered to go to the hospital with him.

## THE SECOND ATTEMPT

At 10:45 a.m., Franz Ferdinand and Sophie went outside and got back into their car. The driver in front of Franz Ferdinand's vehicle was not informed about the new route and went down the original route. As the car reached the Latin Bridge, the plan was to go straight ahead, but the driver had assumed the plan was to turn right. The driver realized his error and had to back up, stopping traffic behind him.

## AN EARLIER ASSASSINATION ATTEMPT

Franz Ferdinand's uncle, Emperor Franz Joseph I, was the survivor of an assassination attempt in 1853 at the hands of Hungarian nationalist János Libényi. Libényi's cause was separating the duel monarchy of Austria-Hungary and giving Hungary independence. Libényi tried to kill the emperor by stabbing him in the neck; however, Franz Joseph I wore a very high collar that blocked the blow. Following the attack, Libényi was captured and sentenced to death.

Princip was there. A bodyguard was shielding Franz Ferdinand and his wife but did so from the side facing the river. Princip was standing on the other side by the row of shops.

Before he fired, Princip hesitated for a second as he saw Sophie; as the rest of the assassins had, he looked at her as an innocent and had no interest in taking her life. But he drew his gun.

Princip fired twice. There was a long moment when no one knew what was happening. The archduke and his wife were stuck in their seats, not moving. Then, as their car started backing up, Franz Ferdinand spurted blood from his mouth. He had been shot in the neck and was bleeding heavily. Sophie saw the wound and cried, "For God's sake, what has happened to you!"[6] She had not realized she was shot in the abdomen. She suddenly collapsed with her face between Franz Ferdinand's knees.

The archduke patted his wife's unmoving head slowly. He moaned, "Don't die. Live for our children." Then his head slumped forward. His bodyguard tried to hold him up. "Is your highness in great pain?" he asked.[7]

"It is nothing," Franz Ferdinand said. He repeated "It is nothing" over and over again until he died.[8]

Despite all the near-misses and mistakes they made, the assassins had managed to succeed in their mission. The archduke was dead, and so was his duchess.

## THE WEAPON

Princip and the other men carried Browning semiautomatic pistols. Princip's model was M1910 and was Belgian-made. This type of gun was used often in combat in both World War I and World War II. After the assassination, the gun was obtained by Father Anton Puntigam, the priest who had given Franz Ferdinand and Sophie their last rites. When Puntigam died in 1926, the gun was lost for nearly 80 years, until it was found and identified by its serial number. The gun now rests in the Vienna Museum of Military History.

## THE TRIAL

The men with the weapons, along with the others involved with the assassination, were found and imprisoned. This included Danilo Ilic, the ringleader, as well as the men who hid the weapons and smuggled the assassins over the border. Only one of the men, Muhamed Mehmedbasic, managed

Austro-Hungarian authorities arrested Princip immediately after the assassination.

to escape to Herzegovina without capture. He made it to Montenegro and was captured by the Montenegrin authorities, only to escape from jail a few days later.

The prosecutor desperately tried to link the anti-Austrian propaganda the students read to the Serbian government. The assassins pointed out that they were hiding from Serbian authorities and were hardly conspiring with them. Grabez said, "I was not led by Serbia but solely by Bosnia."[9] This was bad news for Austria-Hungary, a country looking for an excuse for war with Serbia.

Though the government did not know it then, it turned out Austria-Hungary was correct about a conspiracy. Colonel Apis, the powerful Serbian military commander who had secretly used the Black Hand to push forward the assassination plot, had indeed armed the assassins. However, other Serbian authorities, including the king, were unaware of this.

The trial was two weeks long. Ilic and the men responsible for hiding weapons were hanged. Cabrinovic and Grabez received the maximum sentence a person under 20 could be given: 20 years of hard labor. Cubrilovic and Popovic were each sentenced to 13 years, though Cubrilovic had an extra three years added after insulting one of the judges. Princip also received a sentence of 20 years in prison. At his trial, he said, "I am not a criminal, for I have removed an evildoer. I meant to do a good deed."[10]

While in prison, Princip contracted tuberculosis, a disease of the lungs. He died in prison in 1918, and the Austro-Hungarian government tried to bury his body anonymously. However, Czech freedom fighters found his grave and brought Princip's remains to Sarajevo in 1920. Cubrilovic and Popovic survived and were freed when the war ended in November 1918.

## AUSTRIAN PRISON CONDITIONS

The Austro-Hungarian government imprisoned thousands of Serbs, many for no reason, both before and after the assassination. Most of them, particularly the older ones, died of disease and malnutrition. Tuberculosis was prevalent in these prisons. Men in prison were forced to wear heavy chains, received very little food, and slept in dark, cold, isolated cells that were breeding grounds for disease. Of the 13 conspirators sent to prison, only 5 survived these conditions.

79

# WORLD WAR BEGINS

By the time Princip assassinated Archduke Franz Ferdinand and his wife, Sophie, Europe was primed for conflict. Princip's actions gave Austria-Hungary, which was already at odds with Serbia, the reason it needed to act.

In a matter of days, Austro-Hungarian leaders agreed a military response was appropriate. Now they needed to determine how and when. On June 30, 1914, Austro-Hungarian leaders decided to hold off on any military action until it was clear Serbia was guilty. Austria-Hungary also needed to determine if its ally, Germany, would support military action against Serbia.

Meanwhile, Russian opinion leaned in support of Serbia. Leaders in Russia believed Austria-Hungary had no basis for action against Serbia. They argued the nation of Serbia should not be held accountable for the actions of one of its citizens in a foreign country. Therefore, Russian leaders made it clear they would view any Austro-Hungarian military action as an excuse for that country to expand its territory in the Balkans. Essentially, Russia was clearing a path toward its own military action if Austria-Hungary were to declare war on Serbia.

## AUSTRIA'S ULTIMATUM

On July 14, Austria-Hungary's political leaders declared they would issue an ultimatum to Serbia before taking military action against the country. The same day, they sent a message to German Kaiser Wilhelm II requesting his advice. In his message back to Austria-Hungary, Wilhelm II made no mention of war. But he did call the perpetrators "crazed fanatics" who threatened the stability of the Austro-Hungarian Empire.[1] Wilhelm II also mentioned that nations had a moral duty to take a hard line against anti-monarchists, or those opposed to kings.

The next day, Austro-Hungarian leaders sent a telegram to Wilhelm II letting him know they planned to issue Serbia an ultimatum, and that he may want to mobilize Germany's troops in case Serbia did not accept the deal. Despite this warning, Wilhelm II believed war was unlikely.

Austro-Hungarian leaders met on July 19 to draft the ultimatum's terms. It would be delivered on July 23 at 5:00 p.m. and expire on July 25. The ultimatum had several key points. To avoid war with Austria-Hungary, Serbia would have

An Austro-Hungarian minister delivers the ultimatum to a Serbian official.

to allow the empire to conduct its own investigation of the events of June 28. It would also need to root out anti-Austrian groups within its borders and ban any anti-Austrian propaganda.

To craft its reply, Serbia turned to its ally Russia for help. Russia recommitted itself to supporting Serbia against Austria-Hungary should a military conflict arise. Serbia, with Russia at its back, found the confidence to reply to Austria-Hungary. Serbia accepted some of Austria-Hungary's demands and evaded or rejected others. It agreed to suppress propaganda and clear out anti-Austrian groups if Austria-Hungary could provide evidence of their wrongdoing. However, Serbia would not allow Austria-Hungary to conduct its own investigation on Serbian soil. Doing so, Serbia said, would violate the Serbian constitution and its right to self-rule.

## WAR!

With Serbia's response to its ultimatum in hand, Austria-Hungary had to decide what its next steps were. It decided to partially mobilize its troops. It again sought the advice of its ally Germany. When Wilhelm II got word of the Serbian response to the ultimatum, he was surprised Austria-Hungary had started

## CAUSES OF BRUTALITY

The Industrial Revolution caused considerable change in the nations of Europe, and it had an equally dramatic effect on war technology. Iron, steel, and developments in chemistry and engineering created weapons never seen before on the battlefield. Barbed wire, machine guns, heavy long-range artillery, submarines, airplanes, and chemical weapons were all inventions of World War I. But these advances came with a heavy cost. Germany was the first to embrace the machine gun. In the battle of the Somme, German machine guns killed or injured 60,000 British soldiers in a single day.[2]

mobilizing its army. He believed the Serbian response eliminated any reason for war.

But in Serbia and Russia, preparations for war against Austria-Hungary had already begun. Russia had mobilized 1.7 million troops to support Serbia.[3] Three days after receiving Serbia's reply, on July 28, Austria-Hungary declared war on Serbia.

Austria-Hungary's declaration of war set in motion all the alliances of mutual support crafted in the late 1800s and early 1900s. Russia mobilized its military to aid its ally Serbia on July 31. Germany, obligated by the Triple Alliance to come to Austria-Hungary's aid, declared war on Russia on August 1. Two days later, Germany also declared war on France, which was Russia's ally.

Germany's battle plan, developed by Helmuth von Moltke, required a swift victory over France so it could turn its full military attention to Russia. To accomplish this, German leaders wanted to march their troops through neutral Belgium to Paris rather than take the longer route through western France. But Belgium's neutrality had been declared in the Treaty of London in 1839 and was protected by the United Kingdom. Germany asked the United Kingdom to forget its duty to protect Belgium's neutrality. But the British refused to do so. Despite this warning, Germany invaded Belgium on August 4, expecting little resistance from the Belgian military and hoping its troops could make it through the country before the United Kingdom declared war. However, the Belgians put

# HELMUTH VON MOLTKE

## 1848–1916

Helmuth von Moltke was the chief of the German General Staff when World War I began. He was responsible for Germany's strategy in the war. Born in 1848, von Moltke came from a military family; his uncle also served as chief of the General Staff.

Von Moltke's primary task was to update the Schlieffen Plan for modern times. The original plan called for a small German force in the east to keep Russia at bay while a larger force captured Paris. Part of this force would defend Alsace-Lorraine along Germany's border with France while the bulk of the troops would enter France through Belgium to quickly take Paris.

However, in execution, von Moltke allowed more troops than necessary to fight in the east. With the military split this way, it was impossible for Germany to swiftly take France. Wilhelm II replaced von Moltke just a month into the war. He died in 1916.

up a fight, slowing the Germans. Later that day, the United Kingdom declared war on Germany in defense of Belgium. On August 6, Austria-Hungary declared war on Russia.

The powers quickly separated into two different sides. The Triple Entente, agreed to by France, the United Kingdom, and Russia in 1907, became one side in the war. Serbia, Montenegro, Belgium, Italy, Portugal, Romania, Greece, and Japan would all fight on the side of the Triple Entente powers. They became known as the Allies. On the other side were the powers of the Dual Alliance: Germany and Austria-Hungary. Their two allies, Bulgaria and the Ottoman Empire, joined them to become the Central powers.

## FIRST BATTLES

Between August 7 and September 6, the Allies and Central powers engaged in battles along the French-German and French-Belgian borders. Together, they were known as the battle of the Frontiers and involved two million troops.[5] Battles

## EYEWITNESS TO HISTORY

The German march through Belgium was an astonishing sight. An American reporter was in Brussels, the Belgian capital, when the Germans marched their way through. He described how the German columns started coming down Boulevard Waterloo at 11:00 a.m. on August 20. He soon grew bored watching the troops pass but realized two hours later that the troops continued to appear. "All through the night," he recalled, "like a tumult of a river when it races between the cliffs of a canyon, in my sleep I could hear the steady roar of the passing army."[4] It took German troops three days to march through Belgium.

## THE UNITED STATES ENTERS THE WAR

The United States did not enter World War I until April 1917, after the war had been raging for more than two years. Until that time, US President Woodrow Wilson had practiced a careful policy of neutrality. The majority of Americans did not want to be involved in the war. However, Wilson secretly provided weapons and supplies for British and French troops. Americans stayed isolated until 1917, when Germany sank several US merchant ships. Wilson went to Congress and asked for a declaration of war on April 2. The United States declared war against Germany four days later.

took place in the towns of Mons and Charleroi and the Ardennes Forest in Belgium, as well as the French towns of Mulhouse and Lorraine.

The German march through Belgium had given the Germans an advantage in the first weeks of the war. But by early September, German troops had grown tired while French and British troops had become more confident. The first battle of the Marne put an end to Germany's invasion into France and marked the first battle of the war to include trench warfare.

The battle of the Marne saved Paris from capture, but it also set the stage for a stalemate that would last three years. This futile back-and-forth came to define the fighting that occurred in World War I.

# CAUSE AND EFFECT

The repercussions of World War I can still be felt 100 years after the outbreak of the conflict. The war's brutality, enhanced by the advances of the Industrial Revolution, unraveled decades-long diplomatic ties, shifted borders, and created entirely new nations. Seemingly overnight, imperialism gave way to democracy in western Europe and socialism in the east.

World War I was the bloodiest war in history up to that point. The total casualties are difficult to calculate. Overall, the war caused approximately 37.47 million casualties, including 8.5 million soldiers killed. Russia suffered the most casualties: 9.2 million killed, wounded, missing, or taken prisoner. This represented more than 76 percent of Russia's entire military force.

Germany suffered more total casualties than its fellow Central powers, but Austria-Hungary lost 90 percent of its forces to casualties.[1]

While some may have thought World War I was "the war that will end war," the conflict led to new regimes and new conflicts.[2] The Treaty of Versailles brought a formal end to the war in 1919. It redrew Germany's borders, forcing the country to give up land. Austria and Hungary became separate nations. Two new countries, Poland and Czechoslovakia, were created out of former German and Austro-Hungarian territories. Along the Baltic Sea, the countries of Lithuania, Latvia, and Estonia were carved out of former Russian territory. Serbia, Montenegro, and part of Albania merged to form a new country, which eventually took the name Yugoslavia. Germany's colonies overseas passed to the newly formed League of Nations, an international peacekeeping organization.

## DISGRUNTLED GERMANY

In addition to the loss of territory, Germany also suffered economic and military losses in the Treaty of Versailles. The treaty required Germany to make large reparation payments to France for the damage it caused in World War I. Germany also had to limit its military to 100,000 men, a mere shadow of the force it had at the start of the conflict.[3]

But perhaps the most humiliating part of the treaty was Article 231, which became known as the war guilt clause. This clause required Germany to take full responsibility for starting World War I. The German people reacted strongly to this clause, calling it, together with the other stipulations of the treaty, a "dictated peace."[4] By this, they meant they had no say in the terms of the treaty. These severe terms became talking points for radical political groups in Germany, including the Nazi Party that would eventually rise to power under the leadership of Adolf Hitler and pull Europe into another world war.

## THE SOVIET UNION

One of the most significant changes to the European landscape occurred before the war ended. By 1917, Russia's mismanagement of its war effort and inability to feed its people led to civil

**Adolf Hitler ruled Germany from 1933 until his death in 1945.**

unrest. Workers and soldiers took to the streets of Petrograd, today known as Saint Petersburg, to protest a lack of food. Czar Nicholas II was forced to step down.

After the czar's departure, the Russian assembly set up a temporary government. However, this government faced stiff competition from the Petrograd Soviet of Workers' and Soldiers' Deputies. The two governments battled for control through the summer of 1917. In the fall, the Bolsheviks, a faction of the Social-Democratic Workers' Party, had taken over the Petrograd council of elected representatives. The Bolsheviks staged a coup to overthrow the temporary government, doing so with virtually no bloodshed.

## DEBATING THE TREATY

Delegates from France, the United Kingdom, Italy, and the United States met in France to draft the Treaty of Versailles in 1919. The nations had different objectives for the treaty. France had lost the most in the war in terms of equipment and supplies, and its people demanded Germany pay for their suffering. French Prime Minister Georges Clemenceau also wanted to make sure Germany never built up its military might again. On the other end of the spectrum, US President Woodrow Wilson was less concerned with reparations. Instead, he was focused on forming the League of Nations, an international organization committed to world peace. Focused on negotiation rather than military action, members of the league would mutually guarantee each other's political boundaries and independence.

Under Bolshevik control, Russia became known as the Soviet Union. Soviet expansion began under the leadership of Vladimir Lenin and expanded greatly after Joseph Stalin came to power in 1924. Though allies in both World War I and World War II, the United States and the Soviet Union became bitterly divided through the rest of the 1900s, fighting a political and cultural battle that became known as the Cold War. The Soviet Union eventually collapsed in 1991, following decades of corruption.

## YUGOSLAVIA

As a result of World War I, Slavs were finally able to rule themselves in their own nation of Yugoslavia. It came into existence by breaking from Austria after World War I, merging the kingdoms of Serbia and Montenegro. Finally, the Slavs had a country. But that would not be the end of their struggle. In 1941, during World War II, Yugoslavia was invaded, and the country was split up again. But the Slavs had experience fighting against foreign powers, and between 1941 and 1945 they

### YUGOSLAVIA TODAY

In the 1990s, a number of conflicts were fought between ethnic Serbs and Albanians (or Kosovans), including the Croatian War of Independence of 1991–1995, the Kosovo War of 1998–1999, and the Bosnian Wars between 1992 and 1995. This collection of conflicts and ethnic battles is known as the Yugoslav Wars. As a result of these conflicts, the country of Yugoslavia no longer exists and was changed to Serbia and Montenegro in 2003. Montenegro became independent in 2006. As of 2015, Serbia, Montenegro, and Kosovo are all independent countries—though Serbia disputes Kosovo's independence, claiming the country is a province of Serbia.

organized themselves into the largest resistance movement against occupying forces in all of Europe.

Even after World War II ended, Yugoslavia continued to experience problems. It was annexed by the Soviet Union and became a socialist republic after splitting with the Soviet Union in 1949. There were also ethnic tensions within the country that continued to create violence, especially between Croats and Serbs. The third president of Yugoslavia, Slobodan Milosevic, preached Serbian unity and nationalism. Between 1991 and 2001, the Slavs fought in a bloody ethnic conflict that led to the extermination of more than 140,000 Croatian, Slovenian, and Kosovar people.[5]

## A LASTING LEGACY

The conflict now known as World War I had been building for centuries before 1914. The war did not have a single cause; it was the result of many factors, including nationalism, militarism, imperialism, and a tangled web of alliances.

The legacy of World War I continues to shape the future. Historians will keep looking into the origins of this conflict, hoping to prevent violence of this magnitude from ever happening again.

The Kosovo War (1998–1999) was one of the conflicts in Yugoslavia. It caused thousands of deaths and the destruction of many buildings.

# TIMELINE

**June 28, 1389**
The Ottoman Empire defeats the Serbian army in the battle of Kosovo.

**1839**
The Treaty of London is signed, and the United Kingdom agrees to defend Belgium's neutrality.

**1848**
Franz Joseph becomes emperor of Austria and remains its ruler for more than 65 years.

**1848–1849**
Revolutionary movements in France, Germany, Austria, and elsewhere threaten the royal right of succession.

**1888**
Kaiser Wilhelm II becomes the ruler of Germany following the death of his father.

**1890**
Wilhelm II forces Chancellor Otto von Bismarck to resign.

**1894**
Nicholas II is crowned as czar of Russia.

**1904–1905**
The Russo-Japanese War leads to defeat in Russia and the beginning of a period of social unrest.

**1867**
Austria and Hungary combine to become the Austro-Hungarian Empire.

**1871**
France loses the Franco-Prussian War; Germany is unified as a single empire.

**1879**
Germany and Austria-Hungary sign the Dual Alliance.

**1882**
Italy joins the agreement between Germany and Austria-Hungary, making it the Triple Alliance.

**1907**
Russia, the United Kingdom, and France agree to the Triple Entente.

**1908**
Austria-Hungary annexes Bosnia and Herzegovina, throwing Europe into turmoil.

**June 28, 1914**
Franz Ferdinand and his wife, Sophie, are murdered.

**July 28, 1914**
Austria-Hungary declares war on Serbia, setting into motion a chain of declarations that result in World War I.

# ESSENTIAL FACTS

## KEY PLAYERS

- Kaiser Wilhelm II was the last German emperor and king of Prussia, ruling between 1888 and 1918. He dismissed Germany's chancellor Otto von Bismarck and ruled with strong military dominance.

- Otto von Bismarck was the powerful Prussian chancellor who presided over German unification in 1871. Bismarck was called the Iron Chancellor because of his powerful rule, but he was eventually expelled by the militaristic Kaiser Wilhelm II.

- Vladimir Lenin was one of the main followers of Karl Marx in Russia. Lenin helped start the Bolshevik Revolution in 1917 and was the chairman of the new socialist republic until his death in 1924.

## KEY ALLIANCES

- Treaty of London: This 1839 treaty required the United Kingdom to defend the neutrality of Belgium. When Germany invaded Belgium in 1914, the United Kingdom had to come to Belgium's aid.

- Dual Alliance: Austria-Hungary and Germany signed the Dual Alliance in 1879. Under this agreement, the two countries would support each other if either one was attacked by Russia. In 1882, Italy joined the agreement, forming the Triple Alliance.

- Triple Entente: Russia, the United Kingdom, and France agreed to the Triple Entente in 1907. Each country was required to support the others, but they were not required to go to war on the others' behalf.

## IMPACT ON HISTORY

World War I led to the end of both the Austro-Hungarian Empire and the Ottoman Empire. The conflict also led to the creation of the independent country of Yugoslavia. Following the war, Germany was plunged into a depression that led to a resurgence of militarism. In addition, World War I took place during a revolution in Russia; this event led to the birth of the Soviet Union, which became a superpower in global politics.

## QUOTE

"I am not a criminal, for I have removed an evildoer. I meant to do a good deed."

—*Gavrilo Princip on the assassination of Archduke Franz Ferdinand*

# GLOSSARY

**ANNEX**

To add to one's territory to make one's country larger.

**ARMISTICE**

A temporary stop of fighting by mutual agreement.

**BOLSHEVIK**

A member of the Russian Communist Party that seized power in Russia in October 1917.

**CASUALTY**

Someone who has been injured or killed.

**IMPERIALISM**

A policy in which a country attempts to increase its power through military force and by controlling colonies in other parts of the world.

**MOBILIZE**

To become prepared for war.

**MONARCHY**

A system of governance in which a king or queen rules.

**MOTORCADE**

A procession of motor vehicles, often escorting a prominent individual.

## MUTINY
Refusal to obey orders.

## NATIONALISM
A belief in one's own nation above all others.

## PROPAGANDA
Information used to support a political group or point of view, or to persuade the audience to support their country's participation in a war.

## ROYALIST
A person who believes that monarchy is the best system of government.

## SOCIALISM
The idea that all industries should be owned by the government rather than private individuals.

## STALEMATE
A draw or a position between opponents in which neither side can get an advantage or win.

## ULTIMATUM
A final demand, backed by a threat of punishment if the demand is not met.

# ADDITIONAL RESOURCES

## SELECTED BIBLIOGRAPHY

Clark, Christopher M. *The Sleepwalkers: How Europe Went to War in 1914*. New York: Harper, 2012. Print.

King, Greg, and Sue Woolmans. *The Assassination of the Archduke: Sarajevo 1914 and the Murder That Changed the World*. New York: St. Martins, 2013. Print.

McMeekin, Sean. *July 1914: Countdown to War*. Philadelphia: Perseus Group, 2013. Print.

## FURTHER READINGS

Atwood, Kathryn J. *Women Heroes of World War I: 16 Remarkable Resisters, Soldiers, Spies, and Medics*. Chicago: Chicago Review, 2014. Print.

Fleming, Candace. *The Family Romanov: Murder, Rebellion and the Fall of Imperial Russia*. New York: Schwartz & Wade, 2014. Print.

Lebow, Richard Ned. *Archduke Franz Ferdinand Lives!: A World Without World War I*. New York: Palgrave, 2014. Print.

## WEBSITES

To learn more about Essential Library of World War I, visit **booklinks.abdopublishing.com**. These links are routinely monitored and updated to provide the most current information available.

## PLACES TO VISIT

**Austrian Military Museum**
Arsenal Objekt 1
1030 Vienna, Austria
+43-1-795610
http://www.hgm.or.at
This museum houses many of the most historically important items from World War I, such as the car Franz Ferdinand was murdered in.

**National World War I Museum and Memorial**
100 W. Twenty-Sixth Street
Kansas City, MO 64108
816-888-8100
https://theworldwar.org
This museum includes a facility that holds a field of 9,000 poppies, one for each 1,000 combatant deaths in World War I. The museum houses tanks, weapons, propaganda posters, a realistic World War I trench, and other memorabilia.

# SOURCE NOTES

### CHAPTER 1. THE POWDER KEG

1. Christopher M. Clark. *The Sleepwalkers: How Europe Went to War in 1914.* New York: Harper Collins, 2013. Print. 513.

### CHAPTER 2. THE PEOPLE RISE, MONARCHIES DECLINE

1. Christopher M. Clark. *The Sleepwalkers: How Europe Went to War in 1914.* New York: Harper Collins, 2013. Print. 66–68.

2. "The Last Years of Tsardom." *Encyclopædia Britannica.* Encyclopædia Britannica, n.d. Web. 24 Aug. 2015.

### CHAPTER 3. GERMANY FLEXES ITS MUSCLES

1. "Weltpolitik." *Encyclopædia Britannica.* Encyclopædia Britannica, n.d. Web. 24 Aug. 2015.

2. Christopher M. Clark. *The Sleepwalkers: How Europe Went to War in 1914.* New York: Harper Collins, 2013. Print. 151.

3. "Rumblings of War." *The Guardian.* Guardian News and Media Limited, 7 Nov. 2008. Web. 24 Aug. 2015.

## CHAPTER 4. THE LAST BREATH OF EUROPEAN IMPERIALISM

1. "Crimean War." *Encyclopædia Britannica*. Encyclopædia Britannica, n.d. Web. 24 Aug. 2015.

2. Jesse Greenspan. "The Charge of the Light Brigade, 160 Years Ago." *History*. A&E Television Networks, 24 Oct. 2014. Web. 24 Aug. 2015.

3. Alfred, Lord Tennyson. "The Charge of the Light Brigade." *Poetry Foundation*. Poetry Foundation, n.d. Web. 24 Aug. 2015.

4. "Trans-Siberian Railroad." *Encyclopædia Britannica*. Encyclopædia Britannica, n.d. Web. 24 Aug. 2015.

5. Christopher M. Clark. *The Sleepwalkers: How Europe Went to War in 1914*. New York: Harper Collins, 2013. Print. 144.

6. Gaynor Johnson, ed. *The Foreign Office and British Diplomacy in the Twentieth Century*. London: Routledge, 2009. Print. 132.

## CHAPTER 5. TROUBLE IN THE BALKANS

1. Christopher M. Clark. *The Sleepwalkers: How Europe Went to War in 1914*. New York: Harper Collins, 2013. Print. 82.

## CHAPTER 6. DUELING ALLIANCES

1. "Dual Alliance." *Encyclopædia Britannica*. Encyclopædia Britannica, n.d. Web. 24 Aug. 2015.

# SOURCE NOTES
## CONTINUED

### CHAPTER 7. A CONSPIRACY LEADS TO ASSASSINATION

1. Roberta Strauss Feuerlicht. *The Desperate Act: The Assassination of Franz Ferdinand at Sarajevo*. New York: McGraw-Hill, 1968. Print. 50.

2. Ibid. 75.

3. Ibid. 98.

4. Ibid. 98.

5. Ibid. 99.

6. Ibid. 105.

7. Ibid. 105.

8. Ibid. 106.

9. Ibid. 144.

10. Joachim Remak. *Sarajevo: The Story of a Political Murder*. New York: Criterion, 1959. Print. 214.

### CHAPTER 8. WORLD WAR BEGINS

1. Christopher M. Clark. *The Sleepwalkers: How Europe Went to War in 1914*. New York: Harper Collins, 2013. Print. 520.

2. A. Torrey McLean. "WWI: Technology and the Weapons of War." *NCpedia*. NCpedia, 1 May 1993. Web. 24 Aug. 2015.

3. Christopher M. Clark. *The Sleepwalkers: How Europe Went to War in 1914*. New York: Harper Collins, 2013. Print. 468–469.

4. "The German Army Marches through Brussels, 1914." *EyeWitness to History*. Ibis Communications, n.d. Web. 24 Aug. 2015.

5. "Battles – The Battle of the Frontiers, 1914." *FirstWorldWar.com*. Michael Duffy, 22 Aug. 2009. Web. 24 Aug. 2015.

## CHAPTER 9. CAUSE AND EFFECT

1. "WWI Casualty and Death Tables." *PBS*. PBS, n.d. Web. 24 Aug. 2015.

2. "A War to End All War." *Vision*. Vision.org, Spring 2014. Web. 24 Aug. 2015.

3. "Treaty of Versailles, 1919." *United States Holocaust Memorial Museum*. United States Holocaust Memorial Museum, n.d. Web. 24 Aug. 2015.

4. Ibid.

5. "Transitional Justice in the Former Yugoslavia." *International Center for Transitional Justice*. International Center for Transitional Justice, 2009. Web. 24 Aug. 2015.

# INDEX

# ABOUT THE AUTHOR

Nathan Sacks is a writer and academic writing instructor from Ames, Iowa. He has written five books and currently lives in Minneapolis.